I Give You My Hallelujah	4
ASK SEEK KNOCK	10
THIS IS LIVING	17
WHO YOU SAY I AM	26
My Best Friend	33
VOICES of FREEDOM	41
OCEANS (WHERE FEET MAY FAIL)	50
Little Life (For You Jesus)	57
Made In Your Image	64
WE CAME TO MEET WITH YOU	73
AS THE WORLD SHAKES	81
Heaven Is Our Home	89
WHAT A BEAUTIFUL NAME	97
YOU KNOW ME	105

Hillsong Worship
OUR HILLSONG WORSHIP ALBUM IS THE COMBINED EFFORT OF OUR HILLSONG CHURCH WORSHIP TEAMS TO EXPRESS BOTH OUR PERSONAL DEVOTION AND A CONGREGATIONAL OFFERING OF WORSHIP. EVER-COMMITTED TO RESOURCING INDIVIDUALS, WORSHIP TEAMS AND CHURCHES ALIKE, THE HILLSONG WORSHIP TEAM SEEKS TO BRING SONGS THAT ARE AS DIVERSE AS THE GREATER CHURCH HERSELF IS. OUR PRAYER EACH YEAR IS THAT OUR HILLSONG WORSHIP ALBUM WOULD OFFER SONGS FOR ALL GENERATIONS AND DEMOGRAPHICS THAT ARE DECLARATIONS OF FAITH AND ADORATION.

United, Y&F and Hillsong Kids Teams
UNITED IS COMMITTED TO WRITING SONGS THAT SPEAK TRUTH, CREATE A UNIQUE SOUND, CONNECT WITH CHURCHES, INDIVIDUALS AND ULTIMATELY CONNECT PEOPLE EVERYWHERE WITH GOD. YOUNG & FREE (Y&F) IS THE CREATIVE WORSHIP EXPRESSION OF HILLSONG CHURCH'S CURRENT YOUTH MOVEMENT. HILLSONG KIDS IS THE CHILDREN'S MINISTRY OF HILLSONG CHURCH, CREATING MOMENTS KIDS WILL NEVER FORGET AS THEY GROW IN FAITH THROUGH CHRIST JESUS. UNITED, Y&F AND HILLSONG KIDS TEAMS SERVE IN CHURCH AS A PART OF THE WIDER HILLSONG WORSHIP AND CREATIVE TEAM WHEN THEY ARE HOME. WHEN ON TOUR, THEY ARE ACCOMPANIED BY THE WHOLE HILLSONG TEAM'S SUPPORT AND PRAYERS THAT THEIR MINISTRY WOULD ARREST HEARTS AND POINT PEOPLE TO JESUS, IMPACTING INDIVIDUALS, LOCAL YOUTH GROUPS AND LOCAL CHURCHES.

We are a church committed to inspiring and empowering the authentic worship of Jesus and resourcing the body of Christ.
THERE ARE NUMEROUS RESOURCES WE AS HILLSONG MAKE AVAILABLE INCLUDING INSPIRING TEACHING AND BOOKS BY BRIAN & BOBBIE HOUSTON, CURRICULUM CONTENT THAT CAN IMPACT YOUR CHILDREN'S, OUTREACH AND DISCIPLESHIP MINISTRIES, AND OF COURSE MUSIC. FOR MORE INFORMATION VISIT HILLSONGMUSIC.COM

We are a church that believes in championing the cause of the local church.
HILLSONG CONFERENCE IS ABOUT YOU, YOUR CHURCH AND SEEING GOD'S KINGDOM ADVANCE ACROSS THE EARTH. THIS IS YOUR CHANCE TO LEAN IN, RECEIVE AND TAKE HOME PRACTICAL TEACHINGS YOU CAN OUTWORK IN YOUR OWN CHURCH HOME, FAMILY AND COMMUNITY. IT'S ABOUT BEING REFRESHED AND INSPIRED AND FINDING GREAT STRENGTH AND UNITY AMONGST THE DIVERSITY OF THE LOCAL CHURCH WORLDWIDE. FOR MORE INFORMATION VISIT HILLSONG.COM/CONFERENCE

We are a church that believes in placing value upon womanhood.
COLOUR CONFERENCE, AT THE VERY CORE IS A STRONG HUMANITARIAN MESSAGE. OUR PASSION AND LABOUR IS TO PLACE VALUE UPON WOMANHOOD, SO THAT WE IN TURN CAN ARISE FROM A PLACE OF STRENGTH AND COHESION AND PLACE VALUE UPON FELLOW HUMANITY. FOR MORE INFORMATION VISIT HILLSONG.COM/COLOUR

We are a church that believes in reaching and influencing the world with the message of Jesus Christ.
HILLSONG CHANNEL IS AN INNOVATIVE MEDIA MOVEMENT, BEAMING THE TIMELESS MESSAGE OF JESUS AROUND THE GLOBE INTO TELEVISION SCREENS AND DIGITAL DEVICES TO EMPOWER PEOPLE IN EVERY SPHERE OF LIFE. THIS IS A PLATFORM POSITIONED IN THE HEART OF CULTURE BRINGING JESUS INTO PRISONS AND PALACES ALL OVER THE WORLD. FOR MORE INFORMATION VISIT HILLSONG.COM/CHANNEL

Hillsong Television with Brian Houston is a half-hour Christian television program that features his teaching from Hillsong Church services.
PASTOR BRIAN'S MESSAGES ARE EMPOWERING, PASSIONATE AND PRACTICAL FOR EVERYDAY LIFE. HIS TEACHING WILL INSPIRE YOU WITH THE HOPE, JOY, MEANING AND PURPOSE THAT CAN BE FOUND IN A PERSONAL AND LOVING GOD. FOR MORE INFORMATION VISIT HILLSONG.COM/TV

We are a church that believes in partnership and unity as we advance His kingdom on earth.
THE HILLSONG LEADERSHIP NETWORK IS ALL ABOUT CONNECTING, EQUIPPING AND SERVING LEADERS, AND EXISTS TO CHAMPION THE CAUSE OF LOCAL CHURCHES EVERYWHERE. OUR HEART IS THAT BY COMING ALONGSIDE LEADERS, CHURCHES AND MINISTRIES OF VARYING DENOMINATIONS AND STYLES, WE ARE ABLE TO SEE MORE CHURCHES FLOURISH AND REACH THEIR GOD-GIVEN POTENTIAL THROUGH THIS MEMBERSHIP PROGRAM. FOR MORE INFORMATION VISIT HILLSONG.COM/NETWORK

We are a church that believes in equipping people with principles and tools to lead and impact in every sphere of life.
TO FIND FURTHER INFORMATION ABOUT THE PASTORAL LEADERSHIP STREAMS (INCLUDING YOUTH, CHILDREN, EVENT MANAGEMENT, OR SOCIAL JUSTICE PATHWAYS), CREATIVE STREAMS (INCLUDING WORSHIP MUSIC, TV & MEDIA, DANCE AND PRODUCTION) OR A DEGREE PROGRAM OFFERED ON CAMPUS BY ALPHACRUCIS COLLEGE VISIT HILLSONG.COM/COLLEGE

We are a church in many locations...
AUSTRALIA, BALI, BUENOS AIRES, COPENHAGEN, FRANCE, GERMANY, ISRAEL, KIEV, LOS ANGELES, MOSCOW, NETHERLANDS, NEW YORK CITY, NORWAY, PHOENIX, PORTUGAL, SAN FRANCISCO, SAO PAULO, SOUTH AFRICA, SPAIN, STOCKHOLM, SWITZERLAND & THE UNITED KINGDOM. FOR SERVICE TIMES AND INFORMATION VISIT HILLSONG.COM

TERMS AND CONDITIONS
THANK YOU FOR PURCHASING SHEET MUSIC FROM HILLSONG MUSIC. YOUR PURCHASE GRANTS YOU THE RIGHT TO MAKE ONE COPY OF THE SHEET MUSIC FOR YOUR PERSONAL PURPOSES (PERFORMANCES, WORSHIP SERVICES, PERSONAL STUDY, MUSICAL TEACHING, ETC). HOWEVER THE FOLLOWING RIGHTS HAVE NOT BEEN GRANTED TO YOU:

1. REPRODUCE COPIES OF THE SHEET MUSIC IN WHOLE OR IN PART OUTSIDE OF THE RIGHTS GRANTED TO YOU ABOVE.
2. TO TRANSLATE, ENHANCE, MODIFY, ALTER OR ADAPT THE SHEET MUSIC OR ANY PART OF IT FOR ANY PURPOSE.
3. CAUSE OR PERMIT ANY THIRD PARTY TO TRANSLATE, ENHANCE, MODIFY, ALTER OR ADAPT THE SHEET MUSIC OR ANY PART OF IT FOR ANY PURPOSE.
4. SUB-LICENCE, LEASE, LEND, SELL, RENT, DISTRIBUTE OR GRANT OTHERS ANY RIGHTS, OR PROVIDE COPIES OF THE SHEET MUSIC TO OTHERS. REPRODUCTIONS OF THE SHEET MUSIC CAN BE MADE FOR THE PURPOSE OF CHURCH WORSHIP ONLY WITH AN EXISTING MUSIC REPRODUCTION LICENCE FROM CCLI. FOR FURTHER INFORMATION CONTACT CCLI AT HTTP://WWW.CCLI.COM

FOR FURTHER INFORMATION ABOUT COPYRIGHT OR OTHER USE OF THIS MUSIC, PLEASE CONTACT HILLSONG MUSIC PUBLISHING AT PUBLISHING@HILLSONG.COM

TRANSCRIBED & ENGRAVED BY JARED HASCHEK

I GIVE YOU MY HALLELUJAH

Words and Music by
BECI WAKERLEY &
DAVID WAKERLEY

© 2015 Hillsong Music Publishing.
All rights reserved. International copyright secured. Used by permission.
Tel: +61 2 8853 5284 Email: publishing@hillsong.com CCLI Song No. 7040456

I GIVE YOU MY HALLELUJAH

**Words and Music by
Beci Wakerley & David Wakerley**

VERSE 1:
**You're doing a new thing
Making my heart sing
Bringing colour to this brand new day**

**It's never been clearer
You draw me nearer
You're always with me and You're here right now**

PRE-CHORUS:
**My song a melody
Your perfect love for me
My heart is full of praise
Your love it makes a way**

CHORUS:
**And I give You my hallelujah
Hallelujah for all my days
Jesus take my hallelujah
Hallelujah I give You praise**

© 2015 Hillsong Music Publishing
CCLI: 7040456

PO Box 1195 Castle Hill NSW 1765
Ph: +61 2 8853 5284 Fx: +61 2 8846 4625
E-mail: publishing@hillsong.com

ASK SEEK KNOCK

Words and Music by
BECI WAKERLEY &
DAVID WAKERLEY

© 2016 Hillsong Music Publishing.
All rights reserved. International copyright secured. Used by permission.
Tel: +61 2 8853 5284 Email: publishing@hillsong.com CCLI Song No. 7070124

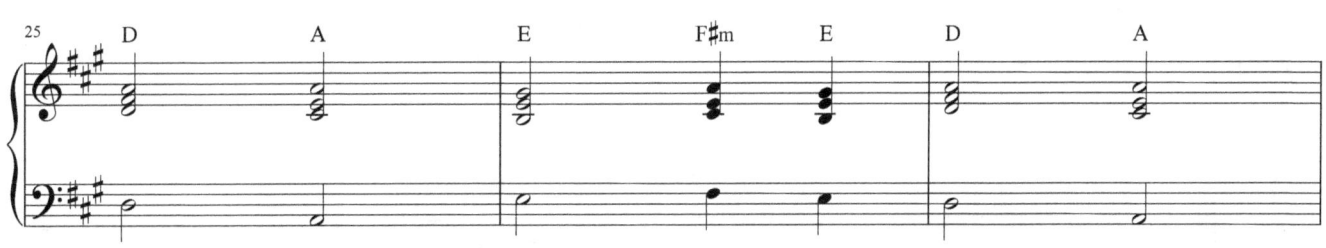

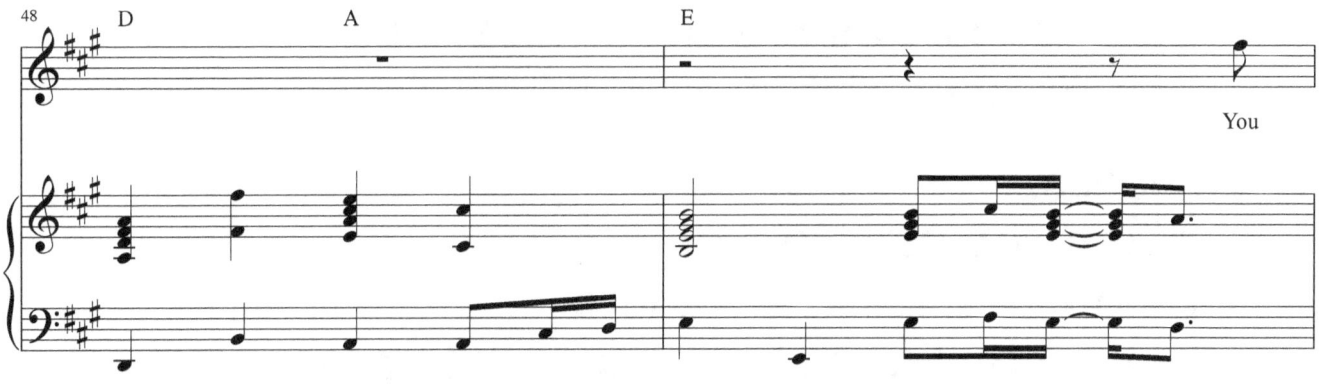

ASK SEEK KNOCK

Words and Music by
Beci Wakerley & David Wakerley

VERSE:
I'm reading my B-I-B-L-E
And this is what it says to me
It tells me that I'm never ever alone

I'm learning how J-E-S-U-S
Came down to us and gave His best
Without a doubt the best friend you'll ever know

PRE-CHORUS:
Our God knows exactly what I need
So I remember this

CHORUS:
When you ask He cares
When you seek He's there
When you knock knock knock knock knock
God opens up the door

© 2016 Hillsong Music Publishing
CCLI: 7070124

PO Box 1195 Castle Hill NSW 1765
Ph: +61 2 8853 5284 Fx: +61 2 8846 4625
E-mail: publishing@hillsong.com

THIS IS LIVING

Words and Music by
JOEL DAVIES &
AODHAN KING

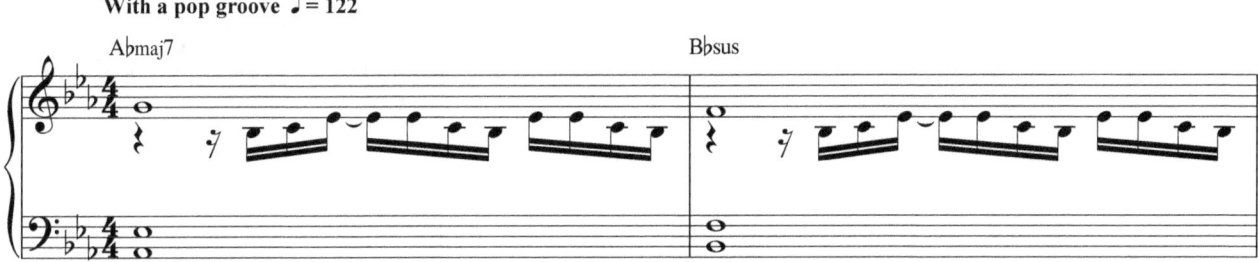

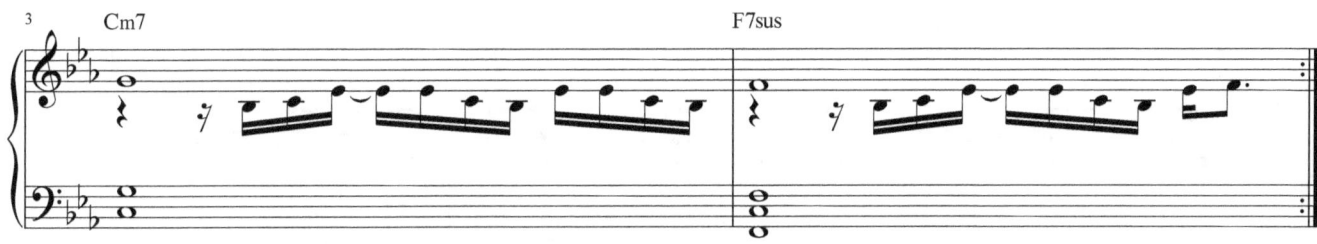

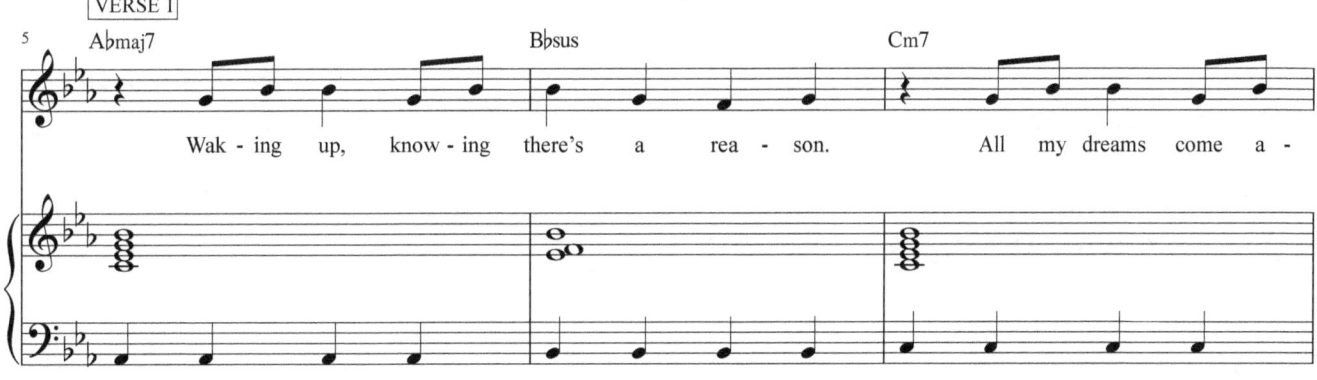

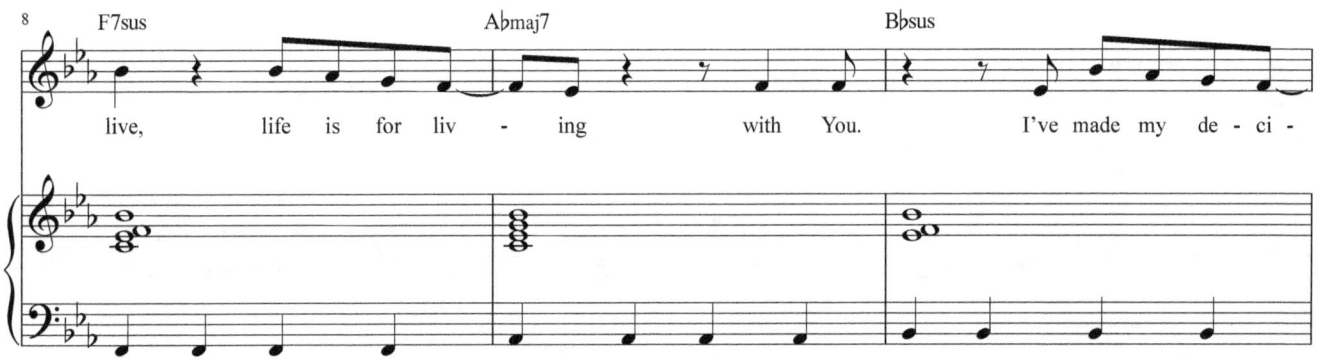

© 2014 Hillsong Music Publishing.
All rights reserved. International copyright secured. Used by permission.
Tel: +61 2 8853 5284 Email: publishing@hillsong.com CCLI Song No. 7032393

THIS IS LIVING

**Words and Music by
Joel Davies & Aodhan King**

VERSE 1:
Waking up knowing there's a reason
All my dreams come alive
Life is for living with You
I've made my decision

VERSE 2:
You lift me up fill my eyes with wonder
Forever young in Your love
This freedom's untainted with You
No moment is wasted

PRE-CHORUS:
See the sun now bursting through the clouds
Black and white turn to colour all around
All is new in the Saviour I am found
This is living now

© 2014 Hillsong Music Publishing
CCLI: 7032393

PO Box 1195 Castle Hill NSW 1765
Ph: +61 2 8853 5284 Fx: +61 2 8846 4625
E-mail: publishing@hillsong.com

VERSE 3:
You lead the way
God You're right beside me
In Your love I'm complete
There's nothing like living with You
This life You created I choose

CHORUS:
You take me higher than I've been before
It's Your perfect love that sees me soar
God Your freedom is an open door
You are everything I want and more

© 2014 Hillsong Music Publishing
CCLI: 7032393

PO Box 1195 Castle Hill NSW 1765
Ph: +61 2 8853 5284 Fx: +61 2 8846 4625
E-mail: publishing@hillsong.com

WHO YOU SAY I AM

**Words and Music by
Ben Fielding & Reuben Morgan**

VERSE 1:
Who am I that the highest King
Would welcome me
I was lost but He brought me in
Oh His love for me
Oh His love for me

CHORUS:
Who the Son sets free
Oh is free indeed
I'm a child of God
Yes I am

VERSE 2:
Free at last
He has ransomed me
His grace runs deep
While I was a slave to sin
Jesus died for me
Yes He died for me

© 2017 Hillsong Music Publishing
CCLI: 7102401

PO Box 1195 Castle Hill NSW 1765
Ph: +61 2 8853 5284 Fx: +61 2 8846 4625
E-mail: publishing@hillsong.com

CHORUS 2:
Who the Son sets free
Oh is free indeed
I'm a child of God
Yes I am
In my Father's house
There's a place for me
I'm a child of God
Yes I am

BRIDGE:
I am chosen
Not forsaken
I am who You say I am
You are for me
Not against me
I am who You say I am

© 2017 Hillsong Music Publishing
CCLI: 7102401

PO Box 1195 Castle Hill NSW 1765
Ph: +61 2 8853 5284 Fx: +61 2 8846 4625
E-mail: publishing@hillsong.com

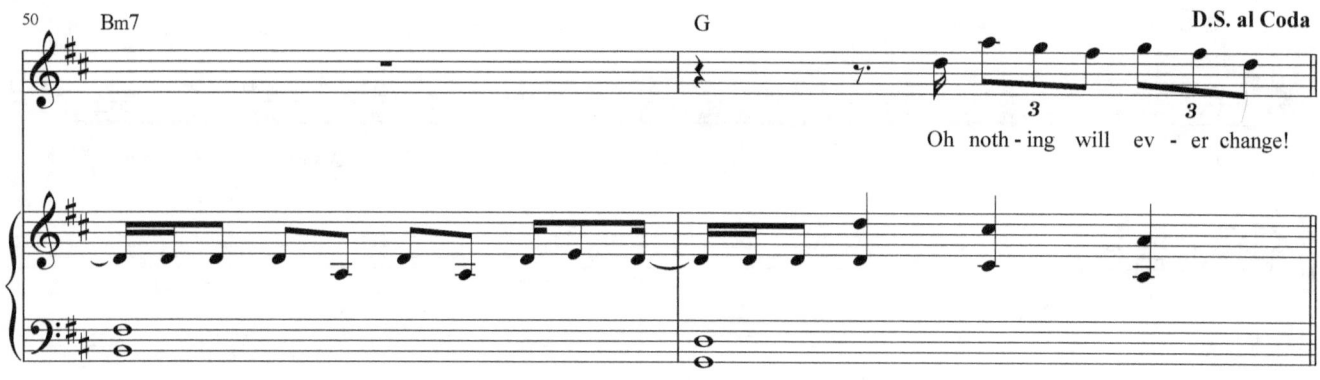

MY BEST FRIEND

**Words and Music by
Joel Houston & Marty Sampson**

VERSE 1:
Have you heard of the One called Saviour?
Have you heard of His perfect love?
Have you heard of the One in Heaven?
Have you heard how He gave His Son?

PRE-CHORUS:
'Cause I have found this love
I believe in The Son
Show me Your way

CHORUS:
Jesus You are my best friend
And You will always be
And nothing will ever change that

© 2000 Hillsong Music Publishing
CCLI: 3207596

PO Box 1195 Castle Hill NSW 1765
Ph: +61 2 8853 5284 Fx: +61 2 8846 4625
E-mail: publishing@hillsong.com

VERSE 2:
**I believe in the One called Saviour
I believe He's the Risen One
I believe that I'll live forever
I believe that my King will come**

BRIDGE:
**Nothing will ever change that
Nothing will ever change that
Nothing will ever change that**

© 2000 Hillsong Music Publishing
CCLI: 3207596

PO Box 1195 Castle Hill NSW 1765
Ph: +61 2 8853 5284 Fx: +61 2 8846 4625
E-mail: publishing@hillsong.com

VOICES OF FREEDOM

**Words and Music by
Ben Banton, Joshua Banton & Scott Groom**

VERSE 1:
My heart was captured
Sin held me captive
Now 'cause of You God I'm set free
I feel like dancing
I can't help moving
I got this crazy joy creeping up in me

PRE-CHORUS:
Woah
Let's wake the city up
Woah

© 2017 Hillsong Music Publishing
CCLI: 7099495

PO Box 1195 Castle Hill NSW 1765
Ph: +61 2 8853 5284 Fx: +61 2 8846 4625
E-mail: publishing@hillsong.com

CHORUS:
When the crowds go home
And the hype dies down
We will sing 'cause we're unashamed
Just like Paul and Silas
We're not staying quiet
Whenever we praise
We sing with voices of freedom
We sing with voices of freedom

VERSE 2:
You give me purpose
You keep Your promise
I hear Your Spirit call to me
To be the difference
To live for Jesus
To shine a light now for all to see

BRIDGE:
Whatever the calling
Whatever the moment
We'll sing
Whatever the calling
Whatever the moment
We'll sing with voices of freedom

© 2017 Hillsong Music Publishing
CCLI: 7099495

PO Box 1195 Castle Hill NSW 1765
Ph: +61 2 8853 5284 Fx: +61 2 8846 4625
E-mail: publishing@hillsong.com

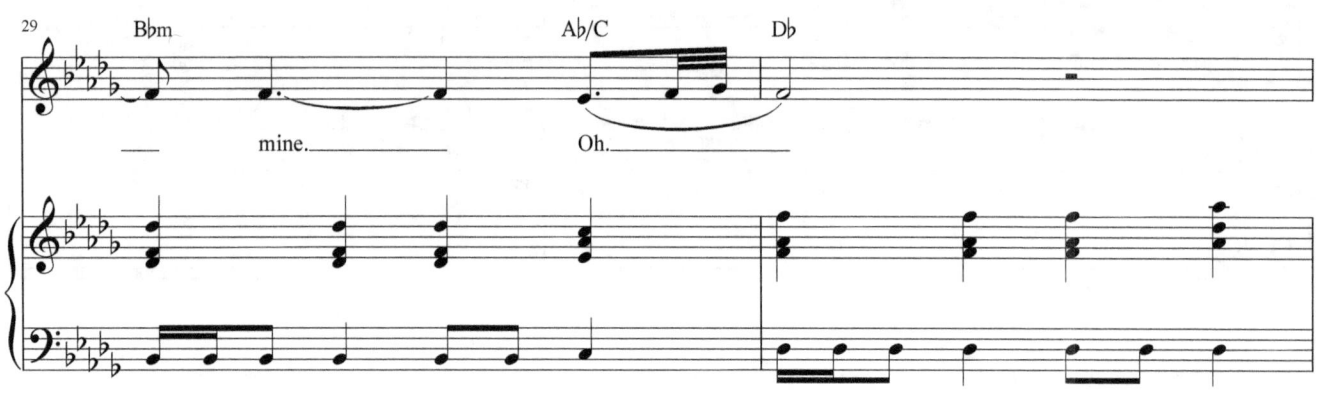

OCEANS
(WHERE FEET MAY FAIL)

Words and Music by
Matt Crocker, Joel Houston & Salomon Ligthelm

VERSE 1:
You call me out upon the waters
The great unknown where feet may fail
And there I find You in the mystery
In oceans deep my faith will stand

CHORUS:
I will call upon Your Name
And keep my eyes above the waves
When oceans rise
My soul will rest in Your embrace
For I am Yours and You are mine

VERSE 2:
Your grace abounds in deepest waters
Your sovereign hand will be my guide
Where feet may fail and fear surrounds me
You've never failed and You won't start now

© 2012 Hillsong Music Publishing
CCLI: 6428767

PO Box 1195 Castle Hill NSW 1765
Ph: +61 2 8853 5284 Fx: +61 2 8846 4625
E-mail: publishing@hillsong.com

BRIDGE:
Spirit lead me where my trust is without borders
Let me walk upon the waters
Wherever You would call me
Take me deeper than my feet could ever wander
And my faith will be made stronger
In the presence of my Saviour

LAST CHORUS:
I will call upon Your Name
Keep my eyes above the waves
My soul will rest in Your embrace
I am Yours and You are mine

© 2012 Hillsong Music Publishing
CCLI: 6428767

PO Box 1195 Castle Hill NSW 1765
Ph: +61 2 8853 5284 Fx: +61 2 8846 4625
E-mail: publishing@hillsong.com

LITTLE LIFE (FOR YOU JESUS)

Words and Music by
BECI WAKERLEY &
DAVID WAKERLEY

LITTLE LIFE (FOR YOU JESUS)

**Words and Music by
Beci Wakerley & David Wakerley**

VERSE 1:
My little hands together pray to You
My little feet together follow You
I lift my eyes and look to You
And my heart will love You

CHORUS:
God You are my Father
Jesus Christ my friend
Holy Spirit You help me on my way

BRIDGE:
I believe in Your Name
I believe in Your word
I believe in the cross
I am free

© 2015 Hillsong Music Publishing
CCLI: 7107107

PO Box 1195 Castle Hill NSW 1765
Ph: +61 2 8853 5284 Fx: +61 2 8846 4625
E-mail: publishing@hillsong.com

TAG:
**This life
For You Jesus
Your life
For me**

© 2015 Hillsong Music Publishing
CCLI: 7107107

PO Box 1195 Castle Hill NSW 1765
Ph: +61 2 8853 5284 Fx: +61 2 8846 4625
E-mail: publishing@hillsong.com

MADE IN YOUR IMAGE

**Words and Music by
Ben Banton, Joshua Banton & David Wakerley**

VERSE 1:
These hands these feet
These eyes that seek
To find their hope in You
Are made in Your image
I'm made in Your image

This heart that beats
This mouth that speaks
More and more like You
Are made in Your image
I'm made in Your image

PRE-CHORUS:
'Cause You are the potter and I am the clay
You're moulding me shaping me everyday

© 2017 Hillsong Music Publishing
CCLI: 7099494

PO Box 1195 Castle Hill NSW 1765
Ph: +61 2 8853 5284 Fx: +61 2 8846 4625
E-mail: publishing@hillsong.com

CHORUS:
I'm trusting in the Lord on the day to day
Picking up strength all along the way
You know what You're doing in me
I'm trusting in the Lord on the day to day
Picking up strength all along the way
You know what You're doing in me
In Your image I am made
In Your image I am made

BRIDGE:
You made me special
You made me precious
You made me wonderful
In Your image I am made

© 2017 Hillsong Music Publishing
CCLI: 7099494

PO Box 1195 Castle Hill NSW 1765
Ph: +61 2 8853 5284 Fx: +61 2 8846 4625
E-mail: publishing@hillsong.com

WE CAME TO MEET WITH YOU

**Words and Music by
NATHAN ESHMAN &
DAVID WAKERLEY**

© 2017 Hillsong Music Publishing.
All rights reserved. International copyright secured. Used by permission.
Tel: +61 2 8853 5284 Email: publishing@hillsong.com CCLI Song No. 7099496

WE CAME TO MEET WITH YOU

**Words and Music by
Nathan Eshman & David Wakerley**

VERSE 1:
**Hey! Everyone is here
We got atmosphere
We love this place**

**Hey! Living different lives
But we all unite
For this one Name**

PRE-CHORUS:
**And when we all come together
Your love is making us better
The world will see the truth of who You are**

CHORUS:
**No bigger life than growing up in Your house
Where we discover who we can become
Praising with Your people going all out
We came to meet with You
We came to meet with You**

© 2017 Hillsong Music Publishing
CCLI: 7099496

PO Box 1195 Castle Hill NSW 1765
Ph: +61 2 8853 5284 Fx: +61 2 8846 4625
E-mail: publishing@hillsong.com

VERSE 2:
**Hey! There is more to see
Yeah we got the key
Found in Your Word**

**Hey! I got a heart to serve
Help build Your Church
In Jesus Name**

© 2017 Hillsong Music Publishing
CCLI: 7099496

PO Box 1195 Castle Hill NSW 1765
Ph: +61 2 8853 5284 Fx: +61 2 8846 4625
E-mail: publishing@hillsong.com

AS THE WORLD SHAKES

Words and Music by
BECI WAKERLEY &
DAVID WAKERLEY

© 2014 Hillsong Music Publishing.
All rights reserved. International copyright secured. Used by permission.
Tel: +61 2 8853 5284 Email: publishing@hillsong.com CCLI Song No. 7025100

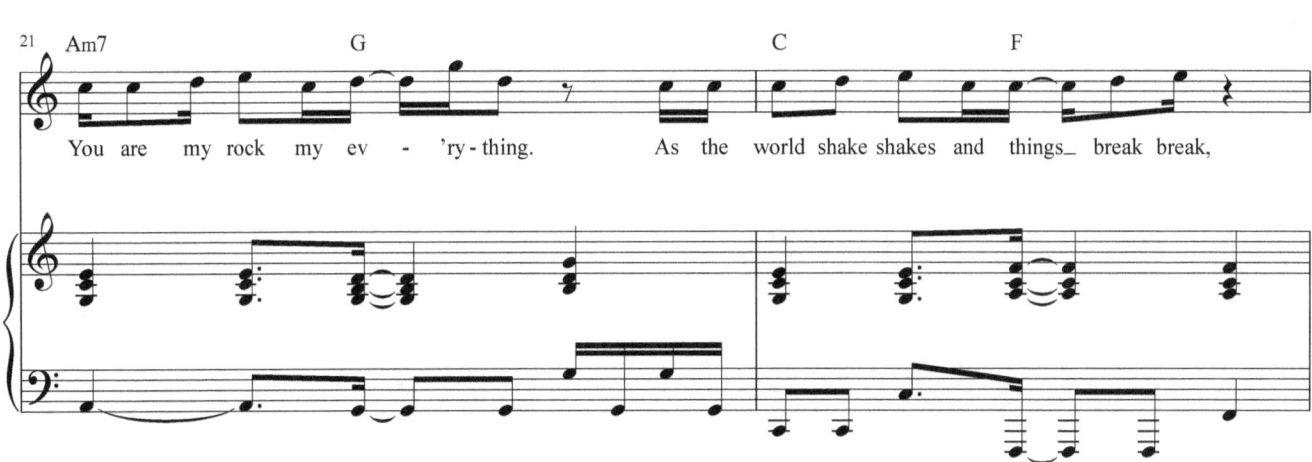

AS THE WORLD SHAKES

**Words and Music by
Beci Wakerley & David Wakerley**

VERSE 1:
No matter what I'm gonna face
Gonna face tomorrow
I build my life on everything You say
You turn the light on now I see
Now I see forever
The path is clearer out in front of me

PRE-CHORUS:
I put one foot in front of the other
Keeping my eyes on You
My life following Jesus
I trust You, I trust You

CHORUS:
As the world shake shakes
And things break break
You are my rock my everything

© 2014 Hillsong Music Publishing
CCLI: 7025100

PO Box 1195 Castle Hill NSW 1765
Ph: +61 2 8853 5284 Fx: +61 2 8846 4625
E-mail: publishing@hillsong.com

BRIDGE:
**As the world shakes
And things break**

© 2014 Hillsong Music Publishing
CCLI: 7025100

PO Box 1195 Castle Hill NSW 1765
Ph: +61 2 8853 5284 Fx: +61 2 8846 4625
E-mail: publishing@hillsong.com

HEAVEN IS OUR HOME

**Words and Music by
BEN TAN, MELODIE WAGNER-MÄKINEN,
BECI WAKERLEY & DAVID WAKERLEY**

© 2017 Hillsong Music Publishing.
All rights reserved. International copyright secured. Used by permission.
Tel: +61 2 8853 5284 Email: publishing@hillsong.com CCLI Song No. 7104925

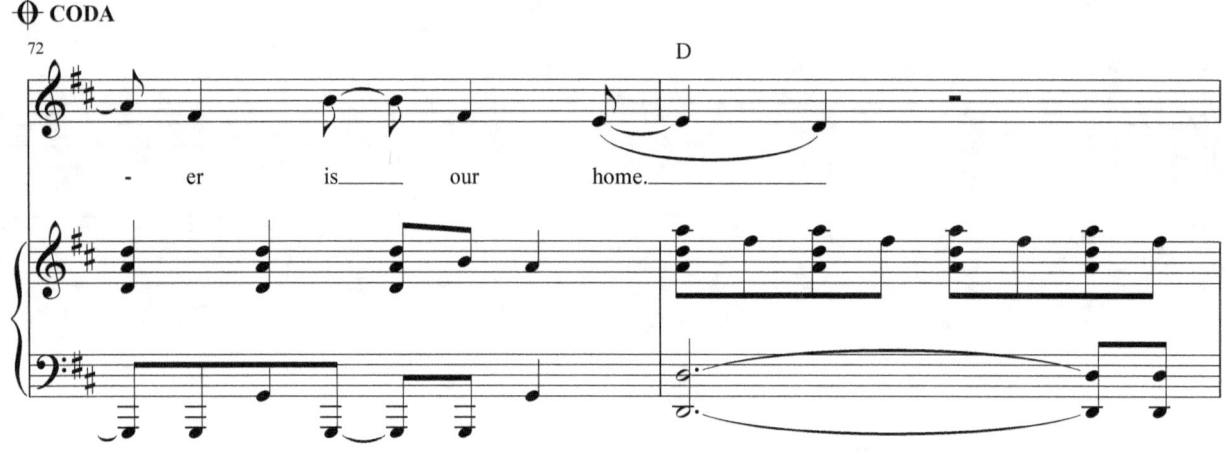

HEAVEN IS OUR HOME

**Words and Music by
Ben Tan, Melodie Wagner-Mäkinen, Beci Wakerley
& David Wakerley**

VERSE 1:
There is a place for me in Heaven
A beautiful truth I can believe in
This great thing I know
The Saviour's on the throne

There's more to this life it's supernatural
I'll set my heart on things eternal
This great thing I know
The Bible tells me so

© 2017 Hillsong Music Publishing
CCLI: 7104925

PO Box 1195 Castle Hill NSW 1765
Ph: +61 2 8853 5284 Fx: +61 2 8846 4625
E-mail: publishing@hillsong.com

VERSE 2:
He's coming back for those who know Him
Nobody knows the hour or moment
We will see His face
His amazing grace

Tears will be gone they'll be no worry
Light of His presence and His glory
We will see His face
Wonderful embrace

CHORUS:
Heaven, Heaven
Forever is our home
Heaven, Heaven
Forever is our home
Forever is our home

© 2017 Hillsong Music Publishing
CCLI: 7104925

PO Box 1195 Castle Hill NSW 1765
Ph: +61 2 8853 5284 Fx: +61 2 8846 4625
E-mail: publishing@hillsong.com

WHAT A BEAUTIFUL NAME

WHAT A BEAUTIFUL NAME

**Words and Music by
Ben Fielding & Brooke Ligertwood**

VERSE 1:
You were the Word at the beginning
One with God the Lord Most High
Your hidden glory in creation
Now revealed in You our Christ

CHORUS 1:
What a beautiful Name it is
What a beautiful Name it is
The Name of Jesus Christ my King
What a beautiful Name it is
Nothing compares to this
What a beautiful Name it is
The Name of Jesus

VERSE 2:
You didn't want heaven without us
So Jesus You brought heaven down
My sin was great Your love was greater
What could separate us now

© 2016 Hillsong Music Publishing
CCLI: 7068424

PO Box 1195 Castle Hill NSW 1765
Ph: +61 2 8853 5284 Fx: +61 2 8846 4625
E-mail: publishing@hillsong.com

CHORUS 2:
What a wonderful Name it is
What a wonderful Name it is
The Name of Jesus Christ my King
What a wonderful Name it is
Nothing compares to this
What a wonderful Name it is
The Name of Jesus
What a wonderful Name it is
The Name of Jesus

BRIDGE:
Death could not hold You
The veil tore before You
You silence the boast of sin and grave
The heavens are roaring
The praise of Your glory
For You are raised to life again

You have no rival
You have no equal
Now and forever God You reign
Yours is the kingdom
Yours is the glory
Yours is the Name above all names

© 2016 Hillsong Music Publishing
CCLI: 7068424

PO Box 1195 Castle Hill NSW 1765
Ph: +61 2 8853 5284 Fx: +61 2 8846 4625
E-mail: publishing@hillsong.com

CHORUS 3:

**What a powerful Name it is
What a powerful Name it is
The Name of Jesus Christ my King
What a powerful Name it is
Nothing can stand against
What a powerful Name it is
The Name of Jesus**

TAGS:

**What a powerful Name it is
The Name of Jesus
What a powerful Name it is
The Name of Jesus**

© 2016 Hillsong Music Publishing
CCLI: 7068424

PO Box 1195 Castle Hill NSW 1765
Ph: +61 2 8853 5284 Fx: +61 2 8846 4625
E-mail: publishing@hillsong.com

YOU KNOW ME

**Words and Music by
LUKE GUEVARA, LUKE SHEPPARD,
BECI WAKERLEY & DAVID WAKERLEY**

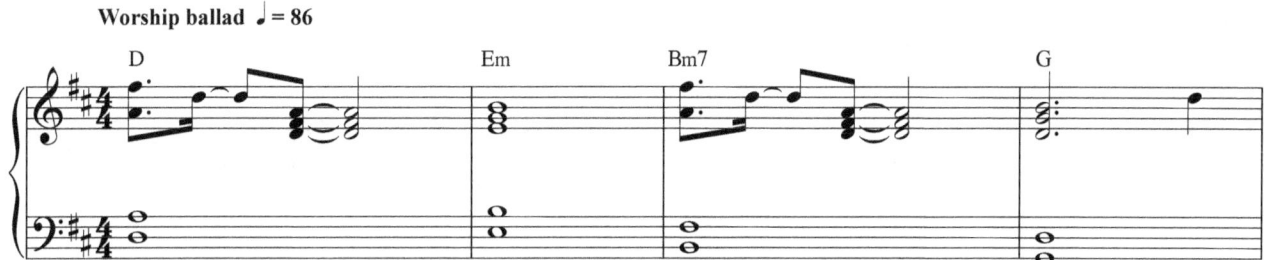

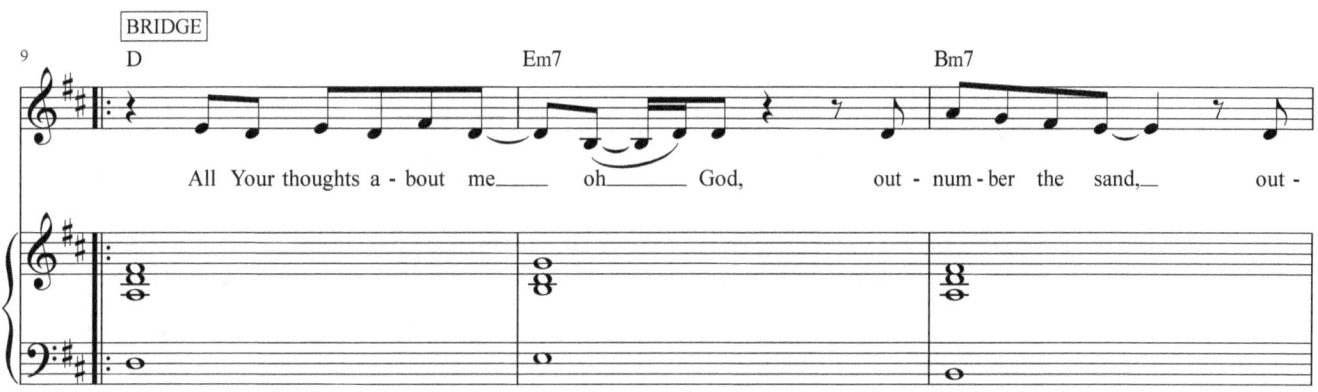

All Your thoughts a-bout me___ oh___ God, out-num-ber the sand,___ out-

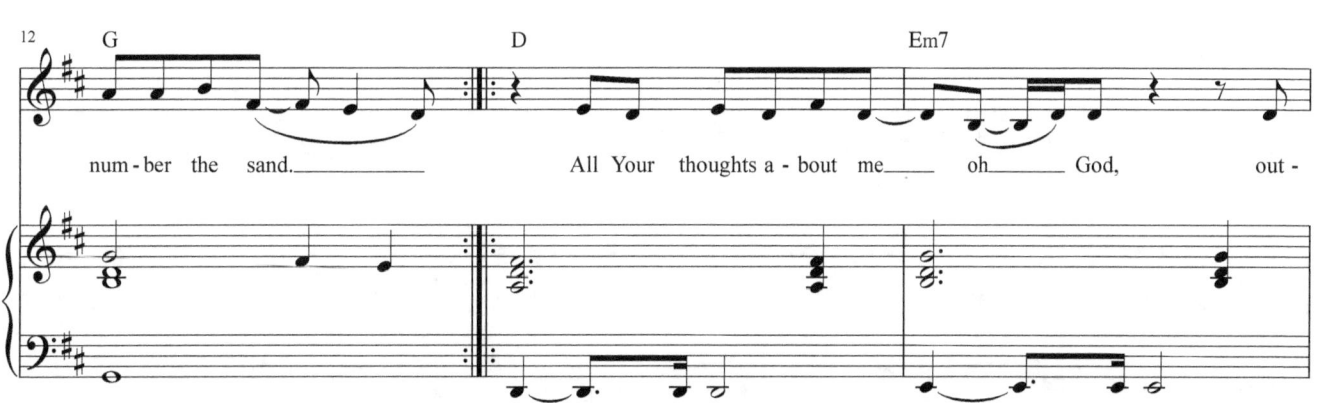

num-ber the sand.____ All Your thoughts a-bout me___ oh___ God, out-

© 2014 Hillsong Music Publishing.
All rights reserved. International copyright secured. Used by permission.
Tel: +61 2 8853 5284 Email: publishing@hillsong.com CCLI Song No. 7025162

YOU KNOW ME

**Words and Music by
Luke Guevara, Luke Sheppard, Beci Wakerley
& David Wakerley**

BRIDGE:
All Your thoughts about me, Oh God
Outnumber the sand
Outnumber the sand

PRE-CHORUS:
You know me inside out
Outside in

CHORUS:
You search my heart
And all of my soul
I live for You my God
You're guiding me home

© 2014 Hillsong Music Publishing
CCLI: 7025162

PO Box 1195 Castle Hill NSW 1765
Ph: +61 2 8853 5284 Fx: +61 2 8846 4625
E-mail: publishing@hillsong.com

ALSO AVAILABLE
from Hillsong Kids

A FULL RANGE OF CHILDREN'S MINISTRY RESOURCE FOR YOUR CHURCH, SCHOOL, VBS, CAMPS OR EVENTS. CURRICULUM MADE BY OUR LOCAL CHURCH FOR YOUR LOCAL CHURCH NO MATTER THE SIZE.

THIS LARGE GROUP SMALL GROUP FORMAT CURRICULUM INCLUDES AGE SPECIFIC MATERIAL FOR TODDLERS, PRESCHOOLERS, YOUNGER CHILDREN, OLDER CHILDREN AND PRE-TEENS. WITH HILLSONG KIDS BIG YOU'LL GET EVERYTHING YOU NEED - HIGH QUALITY MEDIA, PRAISE AND WORSHIP RESOURCES, SMALL GROUP STUDIES, ACTIVITY SHEETS, CRAFTS, COLOURING PAGES AND MORE!

www.ingramcontent.com/pod-product-compliance
Lightning Source LLC
Chambersburg PA
CBHW080808300426
44114CB00020B/2869